A Little Book of

Unspoken History

A Little Book of
Unspoken History

Elif Sezen

PUNCHER & WATTMANN

First published in 2018
Published by Puncher and Wattmann
PO Box 279
Waratah NSW 2298

http://www.puncherandwattmann.com
puncherandwattmann@bigpond.com

A catalogue record for this book is available from the National Library of Australia

ISBN   9781925780147

Cover design by David Musgrave

Cover Image: Elif Sezen

Printed by Lightning Source International

This project has been assisted by the Australian Government through the Australia Council, its arts funding and advisory body.

to my grandparents,
Hatice and Hulki Şanlı

Contents

Ghosts

Remnants

A Poet's Manifesto

One who has perfected himself in the twin arts of remembering and forgetting is in a position to play at battledore and shuttlecock with the whole existence Søren Kierkegaard

Ghosts

On the topic of first parents

She believed in this story. Pompousness of a transparent, glass-like, ice-like feeling that resembled a ghostly disturbance of a shadow. Who put it inside her? An inevitable end of a virgin lack of sense of lost. No. nooooh, this shouldn't have happened. She erased the intimacy of her emptiness with the rubber on the back of her pencil. She wore her slippers and started walking. This scene always used to fall into her mind's eye: Where is it that I cannot arrive? Her battle with carrots, her distrust of potatoes, what about the agony of extreme harmony in the soup stock, what was she going to eat? She threw away the cook book, not feeling hunger at all. She then remembered the dream she had when she was a child. This was a time of exuberance. Lovely hats of parents with their proud naivety, responsible fixture silhouettes, the biggest love ceremony of all times!

She started to call them mum and dad. Thus her worldly clock had started.

Childhood

These societies, herds, get smaller while growing, resembling indefinable, amorphous microorganisms that fill within you when you cackle, so sweet, so adaptable ... They continue to multiply, yet forgetting something, something fragile and perilous: An image of childhood sparkling in silence in the dark river of the collective subconscious.

Gaston Bachelard: "Our whole childhood remains to be reimagined. In reimagining it, we have the possibility of recovering it in the very life of our reveries as a solitary child."

Slap of the morning

Slammed doors are still being heard
Who are they?

Act of grace

A desire fell
into the spirit-core
of a gallows tree
A desire of letting go
surrendering horror
a desire of blossoming

Now the shadow of
this shepherd is lost
His ears are cut
Will the whoosh of
eternity quiet down?

This shepherd dances
in his own requiem now
evaporating into
scent of roses
a circled halo
Will his small self
fade away like this?

One day the shepherd said
'I can see the message
of the union
that is passed on to me
the pain of the owl
the smile of the sparrow
angelic calling of speechlessness
the rope of wish hung on
the air by the yew tree
how everything merges
with nothing

its resolution in the abyss
how souls reach peace
the anxiety becomes a tulip
within palms
a tulip becomes a twinkle
in the apple of the eye

I forgive you daddy'

— says suddenly the little shepherd
as if sawing out his dearest
outer space
a missing town rising above
that sharded ruin
and his magical universe
crumbles upon him

The shepherd reads
written on the entrance gate
in magnificent letters
Unthinkable things can happen

Chronic Fatigue Syndrome

1 Awareness

Now that I am tired
I must open up inwardly like a lotus blossom
yes, I must open my paper-like lids
towards the benign feature of absence
for I will encounter her, in the very bottom:
that archetypal mystic, resembling my mother
by her glance perforating the silvered smoke
my small self will pass away
because I am tired
because fatigue is a lovely trap made to
save my body from its old cage

I learn to become still, yet
teleport simultaneously everywhere

I get rid of the worldly clock
losing beguiling sleep

become a voluntary mute
so I can speak for them

They
surrender their souls
wrapped with flesh and blood and breath
back to where they came from

On land where the power issues reign
and tasteless hierarchy, they find and they choose
the most desert-like spot

for a desert is a home for
repentance

The *anima mundi* is saved here
in discovering the elements,
water, fire, air, earth and ether
through the heart's eye
once again

A lament is sung here,
one which only their forefathers can
hear. So each grief can be freed
like a crumbling piece of bread,
for the animal-smile
hanging on the corner of the wall
is my primitive self whom I once
ignored
this is a new way of loving one's self

For I am fatigued
and my fatigue will explode
like fireworks
upon you

2 Swans

Swans were drifting away on the lake
like forgotten desires, and we were
preparing ourselves for an
ordinary day

3 Metaphysics

Who said angels don't exist?
O angels!
They are hidden in the elixir
of infinity that clears the conscience
of the unspoken
they light the soul-flame in its essence
they secretly orchestrate the flight of
glowworms, electrifying
and dying away towards the East
and towards the West

Whatever East and West means,
this is no secret:
direction does not exist the way we know it
direction is dimensional, not linear

This is no secret:
dying holds you back
not the way you know it
this time keep your angel by your side
and set off on your journey once again

4 The one without an answer

His papyraceous solitude
flowing from the tower of innocence
to the lower planes of the cosmos

tickets tucked in the hands of
the one without an answer

5 The phenomenology of chronic pain

This Aria has no beginning, no end
whereas in the beginning there was the sound
the sound of Love dividing into bits
in between the matter and soul

Over time, the sound transmuted into
moans, arising from hidden wars
and declared wars

Yet today, right here, it
vibrates through the nerve-ends
of a young body

       La Minor   impatience

  Do   black humour

    CRESCENDO   the pain

is so glorious here

First, talk to the pain
Dear pain, what do you want from me?
caress that pain, love it
surrender it to the whole
recycle it
and never forget,
suffering and not becoming monstrous
is a privilege

6 Hope

Close. Close your eyelids
to this landscape
forasmuch as this landscape
— preventing you from being you —
once kept you alive
now it rather destroys

You were saying that this is
the memory of the future
you were rambling about a re-birth
in this future
for you were exceedingly dead
nothingness was tinkling after every death

O Rose-faced child,
the eagle
      passing by the Pacific tangentially,
               pure iron,
    O well of meanings!

You must be empty while you hope,
for what already belongs to you is ready
               to come back to you

"For to its possessor is all possession well concealed,
and of all treasure — pits one's own is last excavated
— so causeth the spirit of gravity"

7 Flying

Forgiveness is what's necessary to fly
also purification
Even purifying from the desire of flying

yet a pair of wings is enough for most
to fly

8 Homecoming

Istanbul Airport is the doorway of my
time tunnel.   No talking!
Act like nothing happened
hereby I discovered the reason
for the lack of bird-chirp
that others dismiss
because I am a bird too
I too forget the necessity
of flight
in all directions of the
forbidden atmosphere of mystery,
simultaneously
'We must declare our indestructible
innocence', grumbles my mum
her eyes staring towards the
beyond-horizons
The birds pollute the new President's sky.
A deaf child disappears from sight
in the alley, after listening to the song
which only he can hear
I call him from behind, with no luck
and find myself
in Melbourne again, inevitably
I chop and add mangos into
my meals again
I forget the malevolence of a
suppressed father image again
I forget my most favorite scent,
jasmine
how holy this forgetting is, I know
for it will pull me back to that doorway
for I'll want to go back home again,

home without geography
without footsteps
how sweet is my abyss.

No memory of fatigue.
I'll again make merry.

9 One more century

In every cross-section of the secondary mornings
there lies a magic

the winking sun, resembling archaic
portraits of women
makes each body solve one more mystery

so that one more century passes.

Sounds

for the absence of memory of home

Only sounds are bartered in this street,
sounds of juvenile vivacity.
But these are not fake, all genuine!

This man is a sound-seller
he would have dreams too
perhaps even some home

with children
sparks of existence within a famine,
he says: 'I'm an ordinary watchman'

deceiving his kids
he has nothing to do with tearing screams,
with busted balloons

he was not seen confessing
to the silence — *of his Forgiver.*
Also, he has nothing to do

with black magic
yet he is perishable
every breath he takes is

unspoken grace, every
smile is inviting
but most importantly

the fate of the sound seller
is to tempt the leftovers
of destitution.

Mortals

'It is too late
for the dead to wake up
for his kissed smile to be
blessed on earth
for his heart to be lit up
by rays not of the moon
for his will to make his truth
out of his error
it is too late
for a pair of eyes
to look for the blue
and find something beyond
for his passion to tinkle in
the body of his beloved
to decide to continue
in the very bottom, very snug
for him to beg for a miracle
it is too late
too late'

— said the religious functionary
as if farewelling the deceased
for his last journey
he wet his hands once more
this time touching the
corpse's forehead
the corpse abruptly blinked an eye
smiling over what was happening
as if making the most of eternity
he whispered.
Goodbye mortals, goodbye.

Footsteps

Where do footsteps lead, these frustrated blind hunters

The homeless woman

There was some light, some dirt
everything else was solitude

the crescent moon used to deliver
violet beams of light, only to

the receptive ones. It used to take
a swing above us resplendently

as if cloaking the vibrations
of puissance. 'Night! Night!'

The outcry of the homeless woman
is a shame in closed hearts

'one homeless, two homeless, three homeless
ten homeless, forty homeless'

The woman forgets to count numbers.
A mind that is purified,

irretrievably — she is the first baby
floundering in the hands named night

Her shadow image closes upon herself
with compassion, unknowingly.

'This is a trap, this is grace'
she is the non-echoic sound in the walls

carrying her lost souls one by one.
Whereas writing history is full

of perils, the woman knows this.
Her hands become

the smoke, the haze, the enigma,
that forgetting revives.

Her hands are now one with absence.

Home

We were made of the same fabric of space
— I was there
as the life-force of little red trees ignored,
as the pressure of wingless wormlike breaths
we were there

Yes, they have lids there
opening and closing with a thinned
fatal silence
they have eyepieces, seeds

Silvery beams of light diffuse
from hands while they're buried
she too will be closed upon herself
and her voice beneath the soil
will be expected to die away

This place is kept clean
with an obsessive compulsive
order of being trapped between two
recollections

A game of joy, its prizes:
balloons, caramels, coloured beads,
dolls — laughing when their batteries are inserted
lemonades, and oh, puzzles of course

I was there
the vertical disappearance of an ancillary image
as a hand, a cavity, a blue,
I was there as a mortal sister and a tree
the night-flower was blossoming intrinsically
my vision became clear: home rebuilt itself.

Coburg Lake

It is time for stillness.
Rainbow aura of the lake washes
the child-faced ones sitting on the bank
with its latent rays
shaking out the ruins with
a word:
Wake up!

While waking up, the eyes
of the child-faced ones become
dazzled, from a light-like
something
but this is no magic, no consolation
from now on the lost babies
cherish themselves

Close!
shouting towards the lake
Close your doors so we can return
and yearn for our true selves

Only after they swallow the seeds
of oblivion
they will remember that
magic flows
through this city
as well

this city ...

blesses blank papers
of a ruled notebook

while it writes its deprivation,
a woman's skirt
blows towards a man

and diffuses as a focused breath
that runs through the yogi, tranquil.

The Turkish bath

Foamed, steamed, speechless
ghosts —

I, my grandmother and a few
others — How nice, angels

are more visible here.
I feel more feminine, and

all women start looking alike
Is this a way to pay one's account?

To whom?
No one knows what's happening here

my grandmother thinks
of boiling potatoes for supper

and yet I am bathing Nietzsche's
Zarathustra in my mind's eye

Look how much
the truth hurts us in this sogginess,

an Ottoman lullaby is strained out of anxiety,
tinkles in my belly button.

I drown in laughter
from the hypothermia of my soul.

Our night afternoon

for Ebru

You say
    'every noun is a gift as long as it trails its hollows'
So we swallow the day's nouns:
       Melbourne   Istanbul   Salonico   Ayvalık
       Bazaar   Cat's-eye   Soap   Pajamas

             We become the evening
             one by one
         we become the blank thing
   You say
   'nothingness speeds the mutation
   invisible blossom   seductive scent'
                      we become nothingness
                      we become the blossom
that seduces

And just then we return into our child body
we are sitting still just so
            to bless our sisterhood?
whilst night blue distills the fear and mystery in the air
and right when our mum was about to press the shutter button
               you and I, our delicate
souls
             are reborn growing up again
we recognise the house we are in again:
        the windows   the carpet
                 plastic roses
       the door that imprisons to the outside

    We don't have a secret remaining

so we no longer wait to grow up
breathing through many a body
we sisters   each other's witnesses
    you and I
while this memory shades off so do we

                        we laugh
                        we hope

Remnants

I remember

I remember the quietness in the house. Frozen, but it has an identity. I'm in the garden, I'm in the living room, I'm in the photo frame. I remember myself everywhere. Also, I don't have a full body as does the sun. I'm tiny, but I have big eyes. I'm waking up, I'm waking up in this place all the time. *Surrounded by chambermaids serving themselves*, in this big house, in this vacuity, I wake up to the truth. I'm dreaming of the warmth, the sincere, dreaming of faraway places, very far though unknown.

A thousand-petal woman

Who am I now?
transparent, motionless
my etheric blueprint is erased within seconds
— else am I a victim of your psychic surgery?
I need that grief back
to complete my circling

this air in which I float
has its direction of flux
this water has its own telling
it hits your face before you hear it
it has its own mind

I am gifted to see this
and yet I forget it again
I meditate upon the deceased again
I inhale Nagasaki,
exhale Hiroshima
you think that I am purified
that's why you call me a Sufi

Whereas I am a confused woman
I have a growing homeless kid within me
she is not me, she is me,
I am.
Thus I learned how to lament on others' behalf
and thus I learned how to claim my light before I die
for I am a thousand-petal woman
opening into universes inside universes

***

Live or die, but don't poison everything ...   Anne Sexton

Kindness is growing
from the well
in which I threw
my memory-container

it is washing over renewed cells
with pure light

magnetising floating words
to the blank paper
— as if seeing them for the first time

it is covering the sky
with a fresh cloud of hope
because kindness
must make our kind
brand new

it must save souls
from their shells
from blind knowledge
and so-called expertise

or else what is poetry
if not saving one more life

Dear Immigrants

From the purses of immigrants roll out candies
like not-blessed eye balls, right in front of our feet.

And just about to say Well Come, we
rather remain silent
as if ripping out the tree roots from its soil
or sending the raindrops back where they came from
locking up our dear immigrants, outside
till we lock ourselves into cells,
shrinking more and more.

Their bodies

are carved on _ _e — *contemplation*
as water, once flowing towards
another Antarctic
as a ruin of hcl_y residuals
failing to become soulless
and have failed to be consumed
by inebriated modernisations.

They were once Lemurians
hypothetical root-race of nothingness
they hid their passions and retributions
within starseed crystals,
a wordless speech inherited from
one generation to the other
for poetry is formless, when the suppressed
is being spat out like that.

Their freedom is our terror
our freedom is a nonsense play of the future

Their chanting can be heard
in the time of full moon.
Our non-clairaudient humanity
deaf, senseless, colossal
cannot hear a cantus of a sensitive soul

Their glances are imprinted within fixations of
our children, born and unborn
with each abuse another child will be sprouting,
starting a gamble as an illusionary devil.

Constellations

for Carl Jung

There is nothing tragic about an Accord where it does not destroy
not even with death it destroys, for death is a second shade
in a microcosm macrocosm opens
                              a petite flower
roaring like a laughter of surprise
between dreamscapes of Africa, India, Native America
it returns to this man his ancient.
Beautiful Philemon murmurs on him
makes him speak out:
"the goal is not the heights but the center"
his God spirit
his human animal
his stellar child
becomes the other within

He says
"man is Abraxas, the creator and destroyer of his own world"
his "effective emptiness" falls upon a mind as snowflakes.
Not boiling star nor faith-cave   a heartspace unfolds
whilst a failed satan tornadoes into himself
Abraxas glows
amongst constellations of psychic wounds

          sit in a cave of whispers
          forget everything and sleep like a cut-head bat
          then carry your speechlessness to the desert
          and remember what is truly yours
          "you must bleed for the goal of humanity"

and he bleeds   a returning child

smiling at a line the poet writes,
Anima is still alive.

The third Frida

for Frida Kahlo

Sitting at the potter's wheel
limbs crumbling and fleet like fairy dust
then you pause
a little deer amongst woods
male-female-human-beast all the same
dripping tears like heated honey
yet that's all you thought you were,
searching for divine water
giving birth to yourself
or imagining your birth sacred
like an Aztec goddess, half-infant half-woman
wrapped in sheets
with ancient coppery blood stains
then you were born, once again
right after your mother's death, but which Khnum
sucks in and blows life
into your mother's womb, your womb
your second half with a shimmering
dissected heart, were all reflections?
as mirrors blinking at each other
from table to floor, wall to wall
— you loved your mirrors yes
an ever-remembered, ever-repeating self returned
half-dead with a landscape
splitting into part day, part night
your ornaments and familiars shiver:
a miniature monkey, a doll, a costume
forbidden light
right there you paint a girl
with an airplane in her hands

between the Teotihuacan pyramids
sitting between sun and moon
the airplane in her hands, flies.

And there it was
swinging between past and present,
life and death, Diego and herself
a ghostly image of two Fridas
the third was absent,
smiling from above.

Our celestial doorway

for Forugh Farrokhzad

Let's meet up in your
imaginary Esfahan
in a city where women glow in *green, head to toe*
when we bend down from
the Khaju bridge, our reflections
on the water turn into nonpoisonous ivies,
a city of secret sovereignty
where bombs won't explode

Once we passed from here
we thought it was a dream
we said we won't come back,
yet on the nib of poets' pens
history is magical.
When I write
we'll be rescued from degenerated crowds,
when you write
we'll prepare for our second birth:

   "Everyone fears,
   everyone fears, but you and I
   merged into one
   before the water, the mirror and the lamp
   and were not afraid"

for *our bodies are our cosmos*
yet their bodies are their caves

A violet flame is lit here
the forbidden prayer, it disinfects the male dominance

What was lost is made visible here
from now on fairytales won't be ignored

What was torn apart is made whole here,
As it should, pure and untouched

My dear Forugh,
we won't be reincarnated to the past,
until there is no war in
our Devic kingdom.

Hyperion of the future

for Friedrich Hölderlin

Your 36 years of silence freed
36 thousand birds from the
hegemony of nonsense,
but you already knew that this
was going to happen, didn't you?

You, an eremite in
Greece, a remnant from
Periclean antiquity

You, created the *Hyperion*
of the future, a little monster
— for them

Your Aias smile
makes me weep

When I grumble
you become quiet
so we both can grow

Your silence makes us live longer.

The Princess Spy

for Noor-un Nisa Inayat Khan, 1914 - 1944

She speaks to herself:
Your soil is rotten
heaven-pap, her mountains lost
the princess spy
Reveal yourself!

Noor at age seven
Her father teaches her the Elemental Sufi breathing exercises

Noor at age thirteen
After her father's loss she becomes a second mother, caring for
her grief-stricken family

Noor at age eighteen
Caught in a laughing crisis while making music with her sister
she loves singing, plays harp and piano

Noor at age twenty
Studies music at the Paris Conservatorium, studies child
psychology
writes children's books,
kind, idealist, hopeful, beautiful woman

Noor at age twenty six
Joins the Women's Auxiliary Air Force,
a secret agent, wireless operator, fights for Britain,
against fascism, speaks perfect French

Noor at ∞
She cups her hands around her dimming light ignored

evaporating in the Gestapo's crematorium
Her last words, *Liberté*

Camille

for Camille Claudel

When everyone is asleep
her eardrums pulse with calypsos

of vampires, vampires of
French evolution, of Rodin's kingdom,

of her cold-hearted mother,
these are fugacious images of the street

— she has no fear
she climbs the slope circling her existence

'Even a street has veins' she thinks,
'we, tiny creatures living in a huge organism,

but my heart beats differently.'
The statues in her studio are more vivid:

remnants, or explosives?
This is how morning leaks in

crystallised on the window glass
rounding the sharp edges,

this is how the No of existence
decomposes:

reminding us of what is forgotten,
effacing what is remembered . . .

Camille sculpts her forbidden love,
Sakountala, diffusing into this planet's matrix

as a softened rock, warm
and fluid

She stares at her *Clotho*
cloaked fractals of hearts diffuse

from this woman into every
direction — she is bitter

as a Pierrot shouting silently
within crowds

No, *Clotho* is not old. She is the
timeless torso of all women existed,

existing.
While she lives, butterflies flit about

from Camille's coffin
as stars of beyond-worlds, in electric blue,

as a first breath,
cherished.

The dual citizen

When we are asleep, we become equal, no passion, no pride, no hope.   Melih
Cevdet Anday

You were not welcome here
— missed your heaven's call
damp walls of the city
closing inwardly
crumbling like fireballs
over its citizens

But you entered,
You . . .
'the little Turkish girl'
as they'd put it
carrying a damaged mother,
a notebook and an intersection
of two countries' solitude
in your luggage

In this realm where the victims
become monsters
you, still pure
illuminated by a distant star
and secretly protected

When they are asleep,
you pray and draw and write
of secret doors within hearths
of gardens hiding the ultramarine
of shrinking intellectuals
of resentful ghosts

of children orbiting absent
images of their parents

With your leaking pen, you cut the
metallic cords of unspoken words
attached to the earth

Like an unspecified plant, you are releasing
your roots, endlessly, while you whirl around
yourself in the blind spot of history

You are entering this territory, once again
this time, you are welcoming yourself
and thus you are being called.

Women in Lapis Lazuli blue

for the silences between meanings

What are all these women doing in this poem?
These women
    These criers
        sprouted from the wilds
            women with lost secrets
        some of them coloured in dark
    as stars appearing and disappearing
            women   in lapis lazuli blue

    Smearing on their ashes to come back
        these death-faced ones

Their hands
        as if revealing the secret of beyond-worlds
                moving over the possible equator of the flesh
            caressing their own incompleteness

            Knitting the abyss like lace
        opening their wounds one by one
wounds . . .
        candypink
                home-free
            so talkative
            so bloodless

The wish

We might go to him tomorrow, to the amnesiac lover.   Nilgün Marmara

Whose face is this?
        This tongue   speaking in flowerish
        resembling the river
        reminding of himself on the kitchen doorsill
        Is he a child playing with his gun?
        But he salutes the truth only
        Is he immortal?
        He is.

To unfold   my dear
to unfold what does not belong to you
these are gifts from the Divine
which you receive the moment you ignore them
accept them in famine
accept them as granted wishes
while the world loses its memory.

A Poet's Manifesto

A meditation on timelessness

Ever tried. Ever failed. No matter. Try again. Fail again. Fail better.
Samuel Beckett

This is a loss, a loss. Writing leans itself against me with an
inevitable necessity. At such moments, I must only write and
let go of what needs to be dissolved. This is a must-do, to invite
the novus. In this way I can also free what had just come into
being. The poem I just wrote is an entity in itself, it has a right
to breathe, to be freed from its creator's boundaries if she's not a
connoisseur.
Writing writing writing is such a deprivation from which I build
up an invisible reign on an earth where my footstep doesn't
belong to the spot it steps upon.
More and more I understand that I am a stranger, whose job is to
get lost, to fail in peace and thus to win with no amazement. So
I can give birth to my dearest self, each time even better, even in
livelier warmth.

Yes! I slide towards the tip of the pen
I fall
as if travelling in time
an ultra-subjective transmission
a mysterious path:
direction unknown
∞

most probable disappearance
most probable nonexistence
followed by a sudden rebirth — becoming
beyond the speed of time
perhaps: no space

a miraculous emptiness

On the surface
but this is surface-less-ness
this much non-belonging encourages
the soul-existent to become the place
herself.

While migrating voluntarily
I was pulled back into my body
right after braiding my hair
If I knew it was to be this easy, returning,
would I still become a martyr
amongst these poems? I don't know.
Though I liked it,
I liked it a lot.

Yes, my dear friends
every poet is responsible
for their own timelessness

Dances of the ending season

This is how the sublimity of
the soul permeates the field
then, a wave of the opposite
force permeates,
no crash

Today

Abyss

        is

      w a r m

   today

2+2=5

Consistency is death.
Consistency is death.
Consistency is death.
Consistency is death.
Consistency is death.
Consistency is death.
Consistency is death.
Consistency is death.
Consistency is death.
Consistency is death.
Consistency is death.
Consistency is death.
Consistency is death.

Night Watch

A piece of blank paper and a pen
the poet wants to correct something
the poet tangles with compassion
the poet
          corrects the silence
a light rattle   a laughter
  is heard
a stranger comes in
the poet corrects him too
and that's how a history is erased
This light illuminates an empty body
the evening prayer which you thought as light
                    smiles

Notes

'Childhood': The added two lines are from Gaston Bachelard. *The Poetics of Reverie: Childhood, Language and the Cosmos*, trans. Daniel Russell, Boston: Beacon Press, 1971, p.100-101

'Chronic Fatigue Syndrome': The final three lines of the section 'Hope' are from Friedrich Nietzsche. *Thus Spake Zarathustra*, trans. Thomas Common, Wordsworth Editions, 1997, p.188

'Constellations': The first quotation "the goal is not the heights but the center" is derived from Carl G. Jung's original line in *Carl Jung: Wounded healer of the soul*, by Claire Dunne, Watkins Publishing, 2012, p. 13. "Man is Abraxas, the creator and destroyer of his own world", "You must bleed for the goal of humanity" and "effective emptiness" are also of Jung from the same source, p. 14

'I remember': 'Surrounded by chambermaids serving themselves" are from my poem 'Eight Moons', *Universal Mother*, Gloria SMH Press, 2016, p.16

'Night Watch': was presented as a digital projection as part of my doctoral exhibition *'Night Watch'* at *MADA gallery, Monash University*, 2013

'Our celestial doorway': 'women glow in green, head to toe' echoes "May you be green, head to toe" in 'The Wind Will Blow Us Away', a poem by the Persian female poet and filmmaker Forugh Farrokhzad (1935-1967). *Sin: Selected poems of Forugh Farrokhzad*, trans. Sholeh Wolpe, University of Arkansas Press, 2007. The quoted lines in my third stanza are from the poem titled 'Inaugurating the Garden', in the same book. The phrase "our bodies are our cosmos" is from the diary of my Mother Aliye Şanlı, with her permission.

Acknowledgements

I am grateful for the editorial assistance of John Leonard, and the encouragement and support of this work by Michelle Borzi, Paul Magee and Jacinta Le Plastrier, among others. My sincere thanks to David Musgrave for having trust in my work.

Some poems in this collection appeared in my chapbook *The Dervish with Wings*, as well as in *Rosetta Literatura: International Comparative Literature Publication, Australian Love Poems 2013, Turkish Poetry Today 2015, Cordite Poetry Review, Spoon Bending: A Chapbook Curated by Kent MacCarter, Mascara Literary Review, Plumwood Mountain: An Australian Journal of Ecopoetry and Ecopoetics in collaboration with Rosslyn Avenue Productions*: 'Hope for whole: poets speak up to Adani', 'Dangerous Women Project' – Edinburgh University and 'What happened at the pier: Recalling the journey II' – Lella Cariddi and Multicultural Arts Victoria.